A Mormons Thoughts And Quotes

E. VERL ADAMS

Order this book online at www.trafford.com
or email orders@trafford.com

Most Trafford titles are also available at major online book retailers.

Printed in the United States of America.

ISBN: 978-1-4669-7286-5 (sc)
ISBN: 978-1-4669-7285-8 (e)

Trafford rev. 12/12/2012

 www.trafford.com

North America & international
toll-free: 1 888 232 4444 (USA & Canada)
phone: 250 383 6864 ✦ fax: 812 355 4082

Preface

I started saving some of these thoughts before I went on a mission for the Church of Jesus Chrrisy of Latter-day Saints in 1952-'54.

I don't pretend to be the only one that has thoughts that are worth saving, I just started saving them and it grew into this thing.

Also, there are thoughts that I have collected from others, that I have saved, and I have included some of my favorites.

I have put dates on my latest thoughts. But, I didn't worry about dates way back when I started saving this stuff.

Maybe some of this has subconsciously come from remembering stuff from other people, so I went back and checked on a lot of it on the Gospel Link program for duplication and I was able to get authors for some of them.

I tried to avoid quoting anyone without giving them credit. But, sometimes I have heard others use some of these sayings in their talks after I recorded them.

"I believe that the test of a truly great man is his humility. By humility I do not mean a doubt in one's self, but a curious feeling that the greatness is not in him, but through him."

John Ruskin.

"And when ye shall receive these things, I would exhort you that ye would ask God, the Eternal Father, in the name of Christ, if these things are not true; and if ye shall ask with a sincere heart, with real intent, having faith in Christ, he will manifest the truth of it unto you, by the power of the Holy Ghost.

"And by the power of the Holy Ghost ye may know the truth of all things."

Mormon 10:4-5

"Man finding truth is hopeful. Man knowing truth is wise. Man living truth is holy."

Unknown author.

"A highbrow is a person educated beyond his intelligence."

Arthur Undone.

"The easiest way to become a soloist is by blowing your own horn."

I'm not sure.

"When the moon is fullest it begins to wane. When it is the darkest it begins to grow."

Chinese proverb.

Many think religion is a part of life. To me, life is a part of religion.

I think I did it.

"Many owe the grandeur of their lives to tremendous difficulties."

\Spurgeon.

"There is so much good in the worst of us, and so much bad in the best of us, that it ill behooves any of us, to try to find fault in the rest of us."

Ralph E. Parker.

Caution: Be sure brain is engaged before putting mouth in gear.

"Let us so endeavor to live that when we come to die, even the undertaker will be sorry."

Mark Twain.

"The first and best victory is to conquer self, to be conquered by self is, of all things most shameful and vile."

Plato.

Hell begins on the day when God grants us a clear vision of all that we might have achieved, of all the gifts we have wasted and of all we might have done that we didn't do.

If you had to live with someone just like you for the rest of your life, would you look forward to it as a wonderful opportunity and privilege?

I pray that I will find a wife that will have a good head on my shoulders.

"I do the very best I know how, the very best I can, and I mean to keep on doing so until the end. If the end brings me out all right, what is said against me wont amount to anything. If the end brings me out wrong, ten angels swearing I was right would make no difference."

Attributed to Abraham Lincoln.

My apology; My limited knowledge exceeds my deeds.

Human nature is such that distant wars, earthquakes and cyclones seem less catastrophic than the first scratch on your car.

"Just as fast as we are capable of righteously dispensing the principles of power, of light, of knowledge, of wealth of heaven and earth, just so fast will they be bestowed upon this people."

Brigham Young.

I will serve God, my family and all mankind continually and without reservations. I shall ask no favors or blessings for myself, save it be in righteousness.

I am so thankful that I can serve the Lord in His work at this time and in His way.

I am not in control of any situation. The Lord is in control of everything. And if I stay close to the Lord, He will let me know what is happening.

Receiving revelation through the Urim and Thummim requires a great deal of concentration and consecration of mental and spiritual power.

As we travel the road of righteousness, learn to read the signs and watch for detours.

Success is not in getting rich, but in getting rid of your riches.

Liberty lies in the hearts of men and women. When it dies there, no constitution, no laws, no courts can save it.

The three degrees of Glory; The Celestial, serve God. The Terrestrial, serve others. The Telestial, serve themselves.

Mortality is so fragile, and immortality is so forever.

Keep seeking continual revelation.

Life is too short, compared to eternity, to worry about worldly possessions.

The Lord will judge me by what I did, not by what I say I did.

Fast from wealth and power. Feast on love and righteousness.

Love and faith are the greatest powers on earth, in the universe, or in all of God's creations.

12 July '89.

All that I have and all that I am I owe to, and thank my Father in Heaven for.

21 Feb. '93.

The Spirit that you have with you, and how you do things, is more important than what you do.

28 Sep. '93.

A prayer of the humble; Please Lord, help me that I will not deceive myself, and will not be deceived, about my own importance.

24 Oct. '93.

Those who do not love God should fear Him.

23 Oct. '93.

Set your house in order and develop spiritual power.

9 Jan. '94.

The universe is in orbit, just like our galaxy is.

24 Mar. '94.

How perishable feelings are.

Making the world a better place begins here, and now, with me.

3 Apr. '94.

Do you know how vast the expanse of God's understanding is, compared to the little any one person can learn in a lifetime?

29 Oct. '94.

Fame and fortune are fickle and fleeting, but families are forever.

Those who break God's commandments break themselves.

6 Aug. '95.

Spiritual power beats money power.

26 Oct. '95.

Letting a bad experience with the Church, or an experience with a bad member of the Church, stop you from going to Church, or even to weaken your testimony, is like letting one or two bad apples convince you that the whole barrel is bad.

12 Jan. '96.

I will love my fellow men as much as I can. But, I will align myself with no man or group of men, only insofar as they obey the commandments of God. I will give blind obedience to no man, only God.

25 Apr. '96.

Anything is possible, if it is the will of the Eloheim.

22 Apr. '96.

"Therefore I would that ye should be perfect even as I, or your Father who is in heaven is perfect."

3 Nephi 12:48.

What right do I have to be arrogant?

31 July '96.

"God put me on this earth to accomplish a certain number of things. But, I am so far behind that I'll never die."

Bliss Anderson.

Appreciate; beauty, chastity, Divinity, energy, forgiveness, generosity, health, imagination, justice, kindness, love, magnanimity, nobility, others, people, quality, rest, service, truth, virtue, wealth, etc.

Acquire; balance, confidence, depth, endurance, faith, godliness, humility, integrity, joy, kindness, loyalty, mercy, openness, purity, quietness, reverence, sincerity, trust, unity, virtue, wisdom, etc.

Avoid; bossiness, contention, domination, envy, forcefulness, grouchyness, hate, indulgence, jealousy, kinkieness, loudness, mouthy, narrowminded, oppressive, pushy, quarrelsome, riotous, silliness, troublesome, unkindness, vexatious, worldliness, etc.

1997.

Do I communicate with the spirit of cooperation or with the spirit of contention? Do I help or do I hinder?

2 Sep. '96.

Don't fall in love with a snake.

12 Feb. '97.

The Eloheim communicate via a telepathic internet.

7 Mar. '97.

I need to stop worrying that things won't work out, and have more faith that the Lord will work things out.

18 July '97.

"But before ye seek for riches, seek ye for the kingdom of God.

"And after ye have obtained a hope in Christ ye shall obtain riches, if ye seek them; and ye shall seek them for the intent to do good—to clothe the naked, and to feed the hungry, and to liberate the captive, and to administer relief to the sick and the afflicted."

Jacob 2:18, 19.

Make sure that your priority list is the same as the list the Lord has for you.

20 Jan. '97.

The key to the gift of seership; always use this gift to serve God.

23 Aug. '97.

My goal in life is to live worthy of doing that which I was foreordained to do.

31 Jan '99.

Humility.

"People ask me what my favorite scripture is. I say, 'Well, I have several of them. One of them is this: 'Be thou humble; and the Lord thy God shall lead thee by the hand, and give thee answer to thy prayers,' (D. & C. 112:10). There is no room for arrogance in our lives. There is no room for conceit in our lives. There is no room for egotism in our lives. We must be humble before the Lord. He has so decreed, and if we will do it, He will hear our prayers and answer them with a blessing upon our heads."

President Gorden B. Hinckley.
March 1999 Ensign.

Look for and appreciate the miracles in your life, and don't brag about them.

14 Apr. '99.

Don't flash the cash.

1 May '99.

What will your worldly possessions be worth when you leave them behind.

22 May '99.

Learn how to talk to the Lord, and how to listen to Him.

17 Sep. '99.

Keeping the Spirit of the Lord with you is much more important than listening to the praises of men.

24 Mar. '00.

What you take with you into eternity is much more important that the toys you leave behind.

11 Aug. '00.

What the Lord wants the Lord gets, except with His disobedient children.

1 Apr. '01.

It is an eternal truth that "There must be opposition in all things."

(2 Nephi 2:11)

But, sometimes that opposition (great leadership) comes as a result of a rebellion.

And, sometimes that opposition (rebellion) comes because of good leadership.

If there is no opposition, that we learn good from evil, then our world does not go to the highest degree of the Celestial Kingdom.

2 Sep. '01.

Why do men try to assign a number of years for eternity?

Why do we try to measure space in miles?

Why do we try to limit the power of God to our understanding?

30 Sep. '01.

I pray that I can follow in the footsteps of my Father in Heaven.

7 Jan. '01.

How can I be meek and humble if you're going to be a pushy broad?

19 Mar. '02.

Joyce's epitaph; Here I lie, doing my best to give your ears a well earned rest.

8 July '02.

I am a rich man; I have a good hope of exaltation.

24 Aug. '02.

There are so many things that I don't know, even about myself.

2 Sep. '02.

Be what you should be.

27 Oct. '02.

If you don't need it, don't buy it.

13 Nov. '02.

Give to the poor until you are poor.

26 Nov. '02.

Share the riches of eternity.

21 Dec. '02.

Keep pluggin' along, someday the pain will be gone.

21 Mar. '03.

Don't just pray "Thy will be done." Find out what He wants you to do and do it.

'03.

It is on the darkest, moonless night when you can see the stars in the Milky Way best.

16 May '03.

Endure with patience the chastening of God.

31 May '03.

What was going on before the "big bang" happened?

What is on the outside of space?

Who is the greatest of the Eloheim?

12 June '03.

With so many starving to death, how can I stand by and not help?

9 Aug. '03.

Looking around, experimenting and exploring are fine, as long as you don't break any of the commandments and as long as you repent when you are told to do so. But refusing to repent, or rebelling, will get you a one way ticket to you-know-where.

20 Aug. 03.

Find out what the Lord wants you to do with your life and do it.

23 Aug. '03.

I, of myself, am nothing. What you see is what God has given me.

30 Oct. '03.

What can I do, what am I doing, so that Satan will not destroy me?

4 Nov. '03.

Big money brings big money problems, and I don't need big money problems.

18 Dec.'03.

The finite mind can not understand infinite space, eternity, or the power of God, and remain mortal.

18 Dec. '03.

Don't do anything, even as routine as eating your food, without praying to the Lord about it.

1 Jan. '04.

Don't get ornery with the Lord. There are so many things He is trying to teach us, and so

many blessing He is trying to give us, that it
pays to be patient.

17-20 Jan. '04.

When I make a decision I make too many
mistakes. When I ask the Lord for His help, He
helps me, and He does not make mistakes.

27 Jan. '04.

If I may paraphrase Matthew 26:42; The Spirit
is anxious, but this old body is getting tired and
worn out.

15 Feb. '04.

"Many wealthy people are little more than the
janitors of their possessions."

Frank Lloyd Wright.

What would my Lord have me do today?

20 Feb. '04.

Having a rich life does not depend on having
money.

8 Mar. '04.

When men obey the commandments of God
they prosper.

10 Apr. '04.

If I could only control my mind, and keep Satan out of it, I would be a lot closer to God.

7 June '04.

"Blessed are the pure in heart: for they shall see God."

Matthew 5:8.

The secret for success; do what the Lord wants you to do.

13 June '04.

Prunes; the magic elixir for old age.

21 June '04.

Patience under adversity.

17 July '04.

A good eternal family, that's what life's all about.

19 July '04.

Satan, the Devil, has no friends.

17 Aug. '04.

Patience in pain.

26 Aug. '04.

This last dispensation will not fail.

12 Sep. '04.

Be humble, but don't settle for less than exaltation.

13 Sep. '04.

"Let us here observe, that a religion that does not require the sacrifice of all things never has power sufficient to produce the faith necessary unto life and salvation; for, from the first existence of man, the faith necessary unto the enjoyment of life and salvation never could be obtained without the sacrifice of all earthly things. It was through this sacrifice, and this only, that God has ordained that man should enjoy eternal life; and it is through the medium of the sacrifice of all earthly things that man do actually know that they are doing the things that are well pleasing in the sight of God. When a man has offered in sacrifice all that he has for the truth's sake, not even withholding his life, and believing before God that he has been called to make this sacrifice because he seeks to do his will, he does know, most assuredly, that God does and will accept his sacrifice and offering, and that he has not, nor will not seek his face in vain. Under these circumstances, then, he can obtain the faith necessary for him to lay hold on eternal life."

Lectures on Faith, #6.
Given by Joseph Smith.

Ask yourself, What difference will this decision make in my Eternal Progression?

26 Sep. '04.

I'm just along for the ride, waiting to see what the Lord will have me do next.

11 Oct. '04.

Stay tuned in to the Powers of Heaven.

21 Oct. 04.

Trying to take worldly possessions into the afterlife is only an invitation to grave robbers, and they may count your dead bones as part of their treasurers.

29 Nov. '04.

Character; Helping others when you are in need.

26 Dec. '04.

Trials and blessings; we get a lot more blessings.

5 Feb. '05.

God's greatest happiness comes because of His good family.

20 Feb. '05.

I need to remember the many times I have been helped.

22 Feb. '05.

Was there a Savior for the world our Father in Heaven was born on?

24 Feb. '05.

Sacrifice; Giving up temporal things for eternal blessings.

27 Feb. '05.

DO IT—prayerfully and meekly.

27 Mar. '05.

The reason polygamy is necessary is because so many more men than women don't qualify for the highest degree of the Celestial Kingdom. This is because of unrighteous dominion and because of so much competing with, instead of cooperating with, their fellow men.

But, good men are always ready to give their lives to protect their families and friends from those who practice unrighteous dominion over others.

30 Mar. '05.

We will need a lot of gold and a lot of good men that are friends with God to overcome the powers of Satan.

17 Apr. '05.

Have a good life, a life of service.

24 Apr. '05.

"Next to the power and goodness of God, Satan has nothing to offer."

KBYU 26 Apr. '05.

"Exercise your faith so it will grow stronger."

La Nor Valentine.

Please place priorities in proper Providential prospective.

2 May '05.

The Lord gives us trials, tests, teachings and training.

1 June '05.

OK Lord, what's next?

6 June '05.

I need to remember that there are a lot of people that need food, clothing and shelter a lot more than I need toys.

18 June '05.

Are there any of the countless troubles in the world that can not be solved by the Lord?

2 July '05.

Our progression and learning in this Gospel is in proportion to our sacrifice and faithfulness.

3 July '05.

Men that work through darkness of night to be seen of men, are seen of men, not God.

25 July '05.

Satan thrusts temptations upon us, though we do our best to avoid sin.

25 July '05.

The Priesthood is an Eternal Religious Order.

1 Sep. '05.

The Lord will help me, if I control my pride.

4 Sep. '05.

Always obey the Spirit.

26 Sep. '05.

This is the Lord's work and He has given me this stewardship.

7 Oct. '05.

The problem isn't how many miles there are on this old car, as much as how many bumps it has hit along the way.

7 Nov. '05.

"—God has no sons who are not servants."

H. D. Ward.

If a man has a large family, lots of friends and a good relationship with God, he is very blessed.

10 Dec. '05.

When we get a little money ahead, instead of thinking what do I want to buy for me, we should use the money to help the poor. The Savior commanded the rich young ruler to "—sell all that thou hast, and give to the poor,—" (Matt. 19:21) He also commands us that every man should provide for his family. (D. & C. 75:28)

16 Dec. '05.

Always be humble enough to learn.

18 Dec. '05.

There are so many memories of the good 'ol days that we don't want to change. More of us should remember the good 'ol days so we can avoid "progress" in the wrong direction.

25 Dec. '05.

Sometimes the things that we take for granted, like family, home, country and peace, become much more precious and valuable when we no longer have them.

26 Dec. '05.

Riches are for helping people, not for showing off to them.

30 Dec. '05.

Don't aspire to anything, just serve.

2 Jan. '06.

Try to pattern your life after the Savior by following His teachings and example.

Jan. '05.

The best thing we can do in this life is to work with the blessings the Lord gives us.

15 Jan. '06.

The more power and authority anyone gets, the more scrutiny they get, and the less tolerance there is for mistakes.

17 Jan/ '06.

The Spirit of the Lord can become so strong that the physical body can literally be consumed. Some call this spontaneous combustion of the body. Most of the time the physical body is protected by the Holy Ghost when the Spirit becomes this strong. When we have the Gift of the Holy Ghost we can depend on this protection from the Fire of the Spirit. When Joseph Smith had the Spirit this strong, he literally glowed. This is called being filled with Fire and the Holy Ghost in Heleman 5:45; 3 Nephi 9:20, Mormon 9:20 and in Acts 2:3-4.

25 Jan. '06.

Talk to and listen to the Lord. He has the best fire and life insurance available.

26 Jan. '06.

Learn from your own teachings.

29 Jan. '06.

Is it possible that I am a master link in the chain of events in the plan that God has for mankind? If so, my work is no more important than the other links, when things get going. Every link is important, and no one link is more important than the others, except when a master link is needed, which isn't very often. I pray that I will not be the weak link.

31 Jan. '06.

Having the stagers and stumbles in old age, without a stimulant, is excusable. Just be careful that you don't fall on your—anything.

3 Feb. '06.

Life can not be created. God gives life to our physical bodies when the spirit body enters into it, and a life is taken when the spirit body leaves the physical body. When the physical body is resurrected the spirit body reenters the physical body, never to leave it again.

Life is given to the spirit body when it is born a child of God and that entity called intelligence enters into it. These entities called intelligences were not created, they are eternal. (Abraham 3:18-22).

Life did not evolve from nothing. There are changes within a species, sometimes called selective breeding, but they, life, did not evolve into existence, and they, it, did not "big bang" into existence.

12 Feb. '06.

The rich are responsible for helping others until there are no poor.

16 Feb. '06.

Obey Gods commandments and instructions, and don't try to steady the ark.

24 Feb. '06.

Be careful, and be full of care.

2 Mar. '06.

Murphy's law; "If anything can go wrong, it will go wrong." That doesn't apply to God. He lets thing happen here on earth. But Murphy's law doesn't apply in Heaven, except when God wants it to.

4 Mar. '06.

The reason they don't talk about Jesus's wives, or family, is to protect them, and because He was a polygamist.

7 Mar. '06.

"The best intentions are fraught with disappointment."

Grissum, on C.S.I. on T.V.

PATIENCE!!! Why does it take so long to learn PATIENCE???

12 Mar. '06.

The Lord enjoys playing with numbers.

6 Apr. '06.

Manage your stewardship so that you can help others, instead of paying usury.

14 Apr. '06.

If that's what the Lord wants me to do, that's what I'll do.

21 Apr. '06.

The praises and honors of men are temporary.

The pains of most physical injuries are fleeting.

The joy of exaltation with God is eternal.

The pains of perdition are permanent.

25 Apr. '06.

What do you have to look forward to in the next life?

4 May '06.

We have the agency to obey the Lord, or to not keep His commandments. He will keep His promises for our obedience, and He chooses the consequences for our disobedience.

7 May '06.

I am not worthy of the many wonderful blessings my Lord has given me. I hope I can keep up with His blessings as He pours them out upon me.

19 May '06.

The Lord has given me more blessings that I can tell you about.

21 May '06.

Victory goes to the survivor.

29 May '06.

Pray to the Lord for guidance and direction, then follow through with the instructions He gives you.

31 May '06.

My Lord, my Savior, my family, my friends and my self. Is there anything else that is of any lasting value?

6 June '06.

Soon we will have to make a choice; whether we live God's Law of Consecration or if we go with Satan's Mark of the Beast.

9 June '06.

Beware of the enemy within yourself.

10 June '06.

Father, bless me with the discernment, the inspiration, to know when to be assertive, when to be permissive, and when to be submissive.

24 June '06.

It is sad that so many have struck out in the game of Eternal Life.

27 June '06.

There are not very many that give their life as a martyr, compared to the number that give their lives in a life of service.

27 June '06.

I don't know where this one come from, probably I heard it several years ago, but I have used it several times over the years when talking about people with inflated egos; "I wish I could buy him for what other people think he's worth and sell him for what he thinks he's worth."

30 June '06.

The older I get the more I enjoy resting.

21 July '06.

Each and every person in the world should do the best they can to respectfully help whoever they can.

28 July '06.

Our best blessings come after our hardest trials.

27 Aug. '06.

One of the problems for old fogies, like me, is whether they should have prunes or cheese for breakfast.

8 Sep. '06.

Slothfulness is a disease that putrefies the soul.

12 Sep. '06.

Please don't look so hard for the bad in me, and at the mistakes I made, that you can't see that I repented quite often.

20 Sep. '06.

A definition of humility; an absence of pride.

11 Oct. '06.

Terrorists think their god wants them to murder infidels, even at the cost of their own lives. Christians are taught; "Thou shalt not kill." "Love thy neighbor as thyself."

29 Oct. '06.

We cannot escape the responsibility of the stewardship God has given us.

31 Oct. '06.

Beware of the whirlpool of debt. It'll suck you under if you give it a chance.

28 Nov.'06.

I used to have the attitude towards money; "If you can afford it, get it. I believe the Lord wants us to have the attitude; "When I have sufficient for my needs, give to the poor."

14 Dec. '06.

You know you have been working at the computer too long when you spill your prune juice in the keyboard.

14 Dec. '06.

It's hard to believe in Murphy's Law, which is; "If anything can go wrong, it will go wrong," while you're counting your blessing from the Lord.

19 Dec. '06.

How much should we give back to on our Father in Heaven who has given us our spirit body, our mortal body, the earth we live on, the air we breathe, the plants and animals we use for food, and wants to give us all that He has, if we will follow Him and be like Him?

29 Dec. '06.

Learn to enjoy the joy of a job well done.

12 Jan. '07.

Fulfill your stewardship; do what you were foreordained to do.

18 Jan. '07.

I repent every time I tease my wife,—well, almost every time.

20 Jan. '07.

Live your life so that when you meet God you don't have to pay for your sins or apologize for the mistakes you made. Be the meekest of God's servants and the strongest of His warriors.

27 Jan. '07.

I'm not over weight, I'm just under exercised.

28 Jan. '07.

I want to be a part of this great work my Lord and my Savior are doing.

30 Jan. '07.

All is well in Zion; God is in the Heavens and His work is moving along; the wicked are fighting among themselves and destroying each other; the righteous are learning and progressing, and the Millennium will be here soon.

6 Feb. '07.

Do you think our Father in Heaven ever gets just a little bit tired of hearing His children whining and complaining and making demands?

7 Feb. '07.

Even though my Lord leads me through trials and learning experiences, He will lead me in the path of truth and progression.

8 Feb. '07.

The way to achieve your highest potential is total submission to God's will.

17 Feb. '07.

Don't blame destiny, or anyone else, for your failures.

18 Feb. '07.

Search the depths of your heart, so that when the Lord calls you to go into action, you can humbly serve Him and follow His guidance in performing miracles for Him.

26 Feb. '07.

Being self-centered is a lonely life.

Joyce Adams.

Love is good take-home pay.

Joyce.

Hate is a contagious disease.

Joyce.

Control your appetites and passions, or they will control you.

Joyce and I.

If you don't have charity in your heart, you have a serious heart problem.

Joyce.

Don't put off until tomorrow what you can do today, unless it isn't nice.

Joyce and I.

When you have been into the depths of despair and felt a part of the weight of the load your Savior took upon Himself for your sins, then you can start to appreciate His sacrifice for you and all mankind.

14 Mar. '07.

Meekness without weakness.

15 Mar. '07.

How many people, groups of people, or even civilizations have declined and been destroyed because of thinking they didn't need the Lord, their Creator.

16 Mar. '07.

Situations, good or bad, are usually made better, or worse, by our attitude.

10 Apr. '07.

You know you are getting old, tired and worn out when the best part of the day is a good night's sleep.

11 Apr. '07.

Competing with others to prove your superiority will lead to your destruction. Obedience and submission to the will of God will lead to your progression, growth and winning the greatest prize—eternal life and exaltation in the Kingdom of God.

22 Apr. '07.

I have seventy three nephews named after me, chronologically.

30 Apr. '07.

I think there are secret combinations of secret combinations controlling the oil industry, and a lot of other industries, and governments.

5 May '07.

How are we going to adopt all of these innocent children that died before the age of accountability, who's birth parent don't qualify for the highest degree of the Celestial Kingdom, into families that do qualify for the Highest Degree of the Celestial Kingdom? How many millions, billions, of them are there that need to be sealed into adopted families?

7 May '07.

During the millennium people will be called as seers. They will sit at a computer, gaze into a seer stone and type into the computer the names of children that are to be adopted and sealed to the parents they have chosen to be adopted to, as fast as the names, dates and places of their birth and the parents they are to be sealed to are given.

11 May '07.

I watched an interesting program on T. V. tonight. A couple of ministers were trying to prove the existence of God to two atheists. Of course, neither proved anything to the other. As Shakespear said; "He that is convinced against his will is of the same opinion still."

If you want to know if God is there, you must repent of your sins and go to Him in all meekness and humility and ask Him. He will answer your prayers by revealing Himself to you by the power of the Holy Ghost. Then you must not turn away from this testimony.

8 May '07.

He that endureth greater tribulation receiveth the greater reward, and He that endured the greatest tribulation received the greatest reward.

18 May '07.

How much more is the Lord going to allow the moral pollution to grow, here on the earth He created, before He says ENOUGH!!

29 May '07.

He that is faithful has no need to fear the judgements that are to come upon the wicked in these last days.

9 June '07.

I think that the biggest problems man has is finding the path of humility, meekness and submissiveness to God that God wants him to follow so He can bless him, and to not following the downward path that Satan wants man to follow of pride, rebellion, etc.

14 June '07.

Our Savior atoned for our sins in the Garden of Gethsemane. Then He sealed that atonement when He was crucified.

17 June '07.

Our society is in such a sad condition that when a man offers to help a woman that is obviously in trouble and distress, she runs from him in fear, especially at night.

18 June '07.

When men acts by the authority of The Holy Priesthood After the Order of The Son of God, under the inspiration of the Holy Ghost, and with sufficient faith in our Father in Heaven, marvelous miracles are performed.

22 June '07.

When the Lord gives you so many problems to solve, and so many obstacles to over come, that you need to pray all the time and continually have a prayer in your heart, that's a good indication that you're on track to the Celestial kingdom.

17 July '07.

So many "scientist" are trying so hard to build up their reputations by proving the existence of other being in this universe that they can not hear these being, angels, and Gods trying to talk to them, by the whisperings of the Holy Ghost/ the still, small voice. All they can hear is their own vanity, and Satan whispering to them about how smart they are, as he leads them quietly down to hell for preaching false doctrine.

18 July '07.

It may seem, to some, to be a contradiction that we must learn to become as meek and submissive as a child, even as a Child of God, before we can progress and become a God, even as our Father in Heaven is.

18 Aug. '07.

How much inspiration/revelation can a person receive and talk about before a head-shrink labels him as schizophrenic?

22 Aug. '07.

Life is so frustrating, I keep making mistakes. But, I guess I'll make it through, as long as I don't do things that I know are wrong. It's so hard to repent, sometimes it's impossible to repent, when you deliberately sin.

30 Aug. '07.

I pray that I will be humble and obedient and that I will not deceive myself with illusions of grandeur.

5 Aug. '07.

Be meek and lowly means don't be pushy and don't brag.

15 Sep. '07.

If every member were a missionary and every members heart was turned to their Fathers instead of to their own desires and passions this Church would grow faster.

20 Sep. '07.

Why do some people need to collect Rich Boys Toys?

23 Oct. '07.

Patience and Persistence are required for great successes.

12 Jan. '08.

Don't be day dreaming about the financial blessing you want the Lord to give you while you are "serving Him."

17 Jan. '08.

Faith is the power to telepathically commune with God.

2 Feb. '08.

You know you've got a good marriage, and things have been right for a long time, when your wife teases you about the pleats in the skin on your neck.

11 Feb. '08.

The Lord gives us challenges so we will grow. He does not give us anything that we did not agree to in the pre-existence.

11 Feb. '08.

There are no side effects to good nutrition.

18 Feb. '08.

Satan's Commandments.

1. Thou shalt have no other Gods besides me, my secret combinations, my idles, or money, power, popularity, etc.

2. Thou shalt love me and me only, for I am a vengeful and a wrathful God.

3. Thou shalt not take my name in vain. Thou shalt take the name of the Father in Heaven and the name of Jesus Christ in vain, as much as you want, when ever you can.

4. Thou shalt not keep the Sabbath day holy. That's such a good day to go shopping, to watch T. V. and go camping or just have fun.

5. Thou shalt not honor nor love thy father and mother. Love and honor thy peers, be popular among them.

6. Thou shalt abort and kill babies when you don't want them, or anyone else that gets in your way.

7. Thou shalt commit adultery, homosexuality, sex perversion, especially on children, they are the easiest. Thou shalt dress provocatively to attract and excite the opposite sex.

8. Thou shalt steal as much as you want. What your want is more important than what anyone else wants.

9. Thou shalt bear false witness against thy neighbor and thy family when ever you want, but don't snitch on your friends.

10. Thou shalt covet thy neighbors wife, his house, his car and all his possessions. Get them for yourself whenever and however you can, just don't get caught.

11. Thou shalt not love thy neighbor as thyself. You are number one. Especially, don't love God, He and His commandments, they are too restrictive.

Joyce and I. 17 Feb. '08.

I'm old, a stranger in this world of sin and sorrow, tired of fighting it, sad, confused and anxious to get my work done so I can go back home.

6 Mar. '08.

Before Father in Heaven took me in, I was like a fly speck out there in endless space. Now He wants me to be like Him.

29 Mar. '08.

I do the best I can to understand, remember and record His instructions and commandments. My Lord gives me visitations, inspiration, and sometimes bad circumstances and trials.

6 Apr. '08.

Father, I pray that thou wilt sustain me in my training, trials and testing.

9 Apr. '08.

Let the Lord work things out and be ready to respond as directed by the Spirit.

24 Apr. '08.

Why do people, like connoisseurs, pay $8.00-$9.00 a pound for salmon, then put seasonings on it to change the taste?

3 May '08.

Be patient. Some times we have to wait for the Lord to get all of His ducks lined up. We may even have to wait for Him to launch His navy, before we can get our little rubber ducky in the water.

20 May '08.

I will love all mankind for they are my brothers and sisters. I will serve my eldest brother for He is my Savior. I will worship my Father in Heaven for He is my God.

23 May '08.

There is no one less interesting to listen to than someone that pretends to know more or to be better educated than you are.

18 June '08.

The Lord did not foreordain us to fail.

29 June '08.

Getting a good average for this old man is getting my feet and my head a little cold and the middle a little sweaty while I sleep.

31 July '08.

At all cost, avoid spiritual poverty.

18 Aug. '08.

Don't get upset or impatient with the trials, training and testing the Lord gives you. Moses did there at the waters of Meribah, and look what it cost him.

4 Sep. '08.

I keep thinking I have things figured out, then the Lord doesn't work things out the way I figured He would.

22 Sep. '08

"Adam fell that man might be; and men are that they might have joy."

(2 Nephi 2:24)

So, enjoy a righteous life.

28 Sep. '08,

There will always be dragons to slay and dandelions to dig.

21 Oct. '08.

The Lord always gives each of us the talents, intelligence and strength to do that which we were foreordained to do.

26 Oct. '08.

Homosexuals have every right to disobey the commandments of God; but not in my Church.

9 Nov. 08.

Most of us understand the three dimensions; height, width, and depth. The sad thing is that many, especially the well educated, don't understand that the fourth dimension of life is the spiritual side/dimension of all things.

11 Nov. '08.

Do we count it as an opportunity to grow spiritually stronger when we are afflicted by Satan?

20 Nov. '08.

Eternal riches are measured not by how much we gather in, but by how much we give away.

4 Jan. '09.

Evolutionists can believe they and their family descended from a monkey if they want. Christians believe we are sons and daughters of our Father in Heaven.

23 Jan. '09.

Jesus Christ was born the Son of God; gave us many good principles to live by; performed many

miracles; gave us a lot of good, sound doctrine; lived a perfect, sinless life; was loved and honored by His disciples; atoned for our sins in Gethsemane and died on the cross that we might be resurrected, after many of His countrymen had shouted "Crucify Him" at His trial.
4 Feb. '09.

It's a sad thing when people think politics and popularity are more important than principles.
10 Feb. '09.

Be patient, prepare, be perfect.
15 Feb. '09.

Decisions determine direction, destination and destiny.
5 Apr. '09.

The Lord wants us to learn to have enough self discipline to always do what is right.
5 Aug. '09.

When did our Omniscient Father first know that His son, Lucifer, was going to rebel and lead a third of the host of heaven, His children, to rebellion against Him into eternal damnation?
27 Oct. '09.

If a man thinks, there is no limit.
11 Jan. '10.

O.K, Bishop, how much water am I allowed to drink with my medication before I am breaking my fast?

6 Feb. '10.

God is Eternal. His laws are eternal. God can not change His laws, to satisfy mans desires, any more than He can cease to be God.

15 Feb. '10.

Use the things that get in your way.

21 Feb. '10.

I have a hard time understanding people, usually girls, when their most often used part of their vocabulary is screaming again and again. When I was their age screaming was for extreme pain, fright, or horror movies.

19 Mar. '10.

My God, my Father in Heaven, wants me to follow in the footsteps—the teachings of His Son—and to become like Him, and to receive His Glory.

28 Apr. '10.

May your happy thoughts come true.

25 Aug. '10.

Enjoy being hungry between good, healthy, regular meals.

25 Aug. '10.

Kisses don't cost very much, but they sure are precious sometimes.

26 Aug.;10.

If God is Omnipresent how can anyone, such as married couples in the Highest Degree in the Celestial Kingdom, get any privacy in Heaven?

29 Mar. '11.

I'm getting too old and burned out to keep believing my illusions of grandeur. But, there are still a few more things I have been foreordained to do.

13 Sep. '11.

Those people that spend a lot of time getting money, big houses, lots of cars, and other stuff, need to remember that they would look silly trying to wear more than one pair of shoes at the same time.

9 Oct. '11.

To paraphrase Dallen Oakes; Learn from your mistakes; Repent of your sins.

10 Oct. '11.

Even though our scriptures teach us that we are children of our Father in Heaven, some scientists prefer to believe they are descendants for monkeys.

17 Oct. '11.

Be paranoid enough to be humble.

4 Nov. '11.

"Keep calm and carry on." A British World War 2 slogan.

20 Nov. '11.

Jesus, my Big Brother, is my teacher, my Savior.

My Father in Heaven is the Father of my spirit body.

The Holy Ghost tells me this is true.

10 Jan. '12.

There has been a lot of talk lately about the Capitalistic system as if having money is bad. Compared to Communism, I think Capitalism is a lot better. Monarchy turns out alright some of the time. There are some Capitalists that are selfish and greedy, while there are some Capitalists that are unselfish, generous philanthropists. Having money is not necessarily bad, it's what you do with it that becomes a problem, for some people. There are so many people that do not pass the test of riches.

12 Jan. '12.

Even without the hope of eternal life, Christianity is the best way of life.

24 Jan. '12.

"Happiness comes from what we are, not from what we have."

Elder Richard G. Scott

Patiently, prayerfully, thoughtfully, work things out.

13 Feb. '12.

A good life, a happy marriage comes from loyalty and commitment, not from finding out what you can get away with.

25 Feb. '12.

O.K. kids, here's something for you to think about; I am almost 84 years old now and I am still learning, repenting and growing.

28 Feb. '12.

I want to be a team player on the Lord's team. The Devil and his followers do not work as a team and they can not win, for several reasons.

26 Apr. '12.

Many years ago Frank Sanatra sang a song that said, "The greatest thing you'll ever learn is just to love and be loved in return." This is a great Eternal Truth. The Eloheim build on this truth with Eternal Families. This is the main purpose and doctrine of our Church: Live worthy of the Temple Blessing of having your wife/wives sealed to you, and your children sealed to you, or better yet, having your children Born in the Covenant.

15 Jul. '12.

Who, or what, do you worship? What master do you serve?

12 Aug. '12.

Adjust your attitude!

3 Sep. '12.

If I may paraphrase Robert Burns; "O that some power the gift would give us to see ourselves as our Father in Heaven sees us."

4 Nov. '12.

"And by the power of the Holy Ghost ye may know the truth of all things"

Moroni 10:5.